CATHOLIC
Etiquette
for
Funerals

Kay Lynn Isca

Our Sunday Visitor Publishing Division
Our Sunday Visitor, Inc.
Huntington, Indiana 46750

Foreword

When I was first ordained, a call to the rectory came in around midnight that a parishioner's baby was dying. Arriving at the home, I found police cars and an ambulance parked in the driveway. Upon entering, I saw a baby in a crib whose discoloration made it look like an artificial doll. Then I realized that it was dead.

Commotion was everywhere. There were policemen, doctors, paramedics, and neighbors hurrying here and there. Over in one corner of the room the poor mother of the child sat alone and cried. She sobbed so hard that no one seemed to want to go near her.

Suddenly a woman friend entered the room. Not saying a word, she went over to the mother, embraced her, and then continued to gently hold her. Her calming, comforting effect on that mother was so touching that it brought tears to my eyes. You could see she felt the mother's pain so deeply that the spoken word was out of place. By gently holding the mother in her arms she let that mother's pain surface and enter into her. In a very profound way, experiencing this touching scene was experiencing the precious power of etiquette at the time of death.

Etiquette means having good form. More than this, it translates into knowing what to do, when to do it, and how to do it with heart.

In this discourse on funerals, the one principle above others Kay Lynn Isca emphasizes is that we practice etiquette at its best to help ease the pain of death. It is the deepest pain we can experience, for when a loved one dies, a part of us dies and life's meaning often is called into question, leaving us mystified and overwhelmed with sorrow.

Isca reminds us that the first rule of etiquette is to be sensitive to the best means we can employ for comforting the bereaved. One of her recommendations is to offer to bring food to the bereaved home or to offer to help in cleaning up. She suggests offering to pick up relatives and friends coming in from out of town at the airport or train station. But Isca is quick to add, be gentle in offering help, but don't take control unless requested to do so.

The author reminds us to be extremely careful in our condolences and to avoid banal comments at the funeral parlor like: "He/she looks almost alive," or, "Doesn't it seem as if he/she is just sleeping?" "Such comments," she tells us, "deny or minimize the loss of life, and are considered inappropriate."

In this discussion on etiquette, one common denominator repeatedly cries out at us: "Be respectful." This translates into feeling what the person is going through, looking for helpful ways to support the bereaved, knowing how to act at the wake, funeral, and burial, and knowing how to keep a sacred distance that allows mourning to happen.

Rev. Eugene F. Hemrick
St. Joseph on Capitol Hill Catholic Church
Washington, D.C.

Introduction

*D*uring the conceptual phase of this booklet project, I unexpectedly found myself helping to plan a Catholic Funeral Mass for my brother-in-law. In fact, the day I was to have met with an editor to discuss plans for this booklet I instead spent directly involved in funeral preparations. Though unanticipated, these circumstances offered me additional insight into the unique challenges and graces inherent in Catholic funeral traditions.

Nothing can ameliorate the pain we all feel when confronting death, but we can draw immense comfort from the funeral liturgy and its accompanying traditions. As author and funeral director Thomas Lynch says, "All ritual behavior is an effort to act out things that are hard to put into words. . . . The beauty of Catholic funeral liturgy is symbol and ritual and metaphor."[1]

Thank you for your interest in Catholic funeral etiquette. Whether you are currently mourning or helping to comfort others during their time of grief, I pray that God may grant you guidance. I pray, too, that the information in this booklet may help you participate more fully with your loved ones during a time of need.

Kay Lynn Isca

Catholic Etiquette for Funerals

Some Catholic traditions, customs, and etiquette associated with death have been drawn from the society around us and are thus shared by the majority of Americans. Other common practices and condolence courtesies, however, are uniquely Catholic. These stem largely from Catholic beliefs about life, death, and the afterlife and how these phases are intertwined. Also, as with other occasions, Catholic funeral rites incorporate numerous rituals and symbols to help express our beliefs in nonverbal ways.

Many cradle Catholics may not realize that some of these fundamental ideas and customs are not universally shared by their non-Catholic friends and neighbors. Likewise, many non-Catholics may feel at a loss as to how best to console a Catholic friend or family member when a death occurs. Certain standard phrases and gestures may seem odd, or even inappropriate, when used outside their respective religious cultures. Though some friends will brush off such blunders with an "it's the thought that counts" attitude, it may be disconcerting to others to find that a condolence sincerely offered somehow misses the mark, rather than offering genuine comfort during a difficult time.

Even when religious differences are not an issue, we may be uncertain about particular aspects of funeral protocol, because most of us (at least until a certain age) attend funerals only infrequently. The times we must be responsible for arranging a funeral are even rarer and naturally fraught with emotion.

In this booklet, we will look at issues and customs involved in planning a funeral ceremony for a loved one and consider some of the responsibilities typically expected of the immediate family. We will also examine different protocol and etiquette guidelines for those outside the immediate family circle — friends and family who wish to console the chief mourners. In addition, we will see how different types of situations and circumstances may affect appropriate behavior.

Background

A key distinction between Catholic and Protestant theology concerns the efficacy of praying for the dead. During Protestant funeral services, ministrations and prayers are focused exclusively on the mourners. The prevailing doctrine is that the dead have already been judged and are now beyond need of prayers offered by the living on their behalf. The loved ones left behind are the ones to whom we must direct our charity and concern.

In the Catholic funeral tradition, however, we not only comfort the bereaved, but we also pray for the deceased. The Catholic Church teaches that "though separated from the living, the dead are still at one with the community of believers on earth and benefit from [our] prayers and intercession."[2]

Integral to understanding this link between the living and the dead is the Catholic concept of purgatory. In purgatory — a final purification of the elect after death — we must atone for sins committed during our lifetime.

Catholics believe that by offering Masses, prayers, and good works, the living faithful can help hasten the departed's journey from purgatory to heaven.[3]

As we look now at traditions associated with death in a Catholic family, you can see how these beliefs are translated into specific practices.

Initial Contacts

When a loved one dies, it is obviously a time of great stress and emotion. It may be difficult to make decisions or know what to do, especially if the death is sudden. This is one reason why a priest should be summoned immediately. He can offer not only spiritual support but also practical guidance about what steps need to be taken first. (If a priest is temporarily unavailable, he may ask a deacon or a lay bereavement minister to go in his place.)

Whether we are personally facing the death of a spouse, parent, or child, or whether we are stepping in to assist a close friend or neighbor in that situation, one of the first telephone calls we make should be to the parish priest. If there is any doubt about which priest to call (or whether a non-Catholic minister would be preferred), a brief consultation with the other principals involved may be in order.

Generally, a Catholic survivor will want the support of a priest, even if the funeral itself will likely be a non-Catholic ceremony. Conversely, if the deceased is Catholic and the chief survivors are not, a priest should still be summoned to say prayers over the body. After the death of a loved one, Catholic family members often join with the priest to pray the Psalms and Scripture passages from the Office for the Dead section in the Liturgy of Hours, as an intercession for the one who has just died.[4] When the death occurs in a hospital, especially a large one, the hospital chaplain may be the most readily available priest and will likely step in to lead these prayers and offer support to the family. Given the different theological attitude toward prayers for the dead, we cannot ask a Protestant minister to perform this duty.

Another important task is notifying any immediate family members who are not already present. In most cases, they should simply be telephoned as soon as possible. While it is still preferable to deliver a death notification in person, this proves to be impractical in most families today, with members scattered across the country or even around the world. If we're especially concerned about how an elderly relative or other close survivor will take the news, perhaps we can contact a nearby friend or relative, a priest, or even a police officer who could convey the news in person. Be certain that this is done quickly, though, so that the relative we're trying to protect does not receive a disturbing telephone call from someone else in the meantime.

Who makes these difficult notification calls? This depends on circumstances and the condition of the primary mourner(s). If we are close to the family, we can sometimes be a great help by offering to notify relatives and friends of the death. The important thing is to be sensitive to the feelings of the chief mourners (spouse, parent, and/or child) and use careful judgment. Sometimes the mourners may be too distraught to speak to anyone via phone; at other times it is important to them to notify their family members and friends personally. Don't usurp the major survivor's right to make the calls, but offer to assume the task if asked.

Similarly, if we are in the position of the major survivor, and a well-meaning friend begins to make phone calls (or decisions) that we prefer to make ourselves, we should not hesitate to make our desires known. (This may be especially important if a non-Catholic friend takes charge.) Friends are there to support us, and sometimes they are searching for cues to how they can best help. If we just sit back and say nothing, someone else will probably step in and do things his or her own way.

Another person we will probably want to contact is the funeral director. The priest or church office can suggest a reputable funeral home, if the family does not already have a strong preference. Most funeral homes, especially ones recommended by the parish, have a basic understanding of common Catholic practices. Usually, the funeral home staff will pick up the body from the place of death and take it to their facility.

If the death has occurred far from where we wish to hold the funeral, a local funeral director can be invaluable in assessing the options and arranging to transport the body or remains. Experts caution against dealing with a distant funeral home via telephone, particularly one picked at random from the yellow pages. A good local funeral director will have the contacts and knowledge of pertinent laws necessary to expedite the process and may be able to save you much unwarranted expense.[5]

Organ donation, by the way, is consistent with Church teaching on charity, as long as the body is handled respectfully. In many places, medical personnel may routinely ask the survivors for permission to "harvest" usable organs.[6] By anticipating this request in advance, we may have a better idea of how we might wish to respond when the time comes. Some people find comfort in the fact that parts of their loved one's body can help sustain another's life, but others find it too discomfiting. This decision must be made quickly once death occurs, because timely removal of the organs is essential if they are to be of use to others.

Condolence Courtesies

Condolence flowers are a popular tradition among most Christian groups, although Catholic protocol is a bit unique. When sending flowers to Catholic mourners, we may either send them to the home of the bereaved or to the funeral home, if one is being used (marked "To the funeral of . . ."). It is not appropriate, however, to send flowers to a Catholic church with a similar notation. Why not? In Catholic churches, only a very few flowers, usually from the immediate family, are permitted. This is in keeping with the Catholic preference that religious symbolism not be overshadowed by "secular" symbols. (From a purely practical standpoint, I'm told the custodial staff typically does not like to mess with an excess of leftover flowers either, so many Protestant churches are adopting similar policies.)

While a room full of flowers is a beautiful tribute to the deceased and his or her family, some experts suggest sending a bouquet to the mourners several weeks after the funeral, when the family may be feeling particularly lonely. Others think flowers can express condolences in a way that words cannot express and should therefore be sent immediately upon learning of the death. Some friends prefer to send live plants instead of flowers so that the greenery can serve as a living reminder of the loved one. Any of these can be considerate gestures, unless the family specifies "no flowers" in the funeral announcement. In that case, we need to respect the family's expressed wishes.

A common Catholic condolence courtesy is arranging for a Mass to be said for the soul of the deceased. Catholics can easily arrange this through their own parish or through any Catholic priest. In addition, certain religious orders routinely offer Masses for the deceased, usually providing a card with which to notify the family and a Mass request form to fill out and return.[7] Some families keep a supply of these on hand, to send in when an occasion arises. Although not mandatory, a nominal donation (five to twenty dollars) is customarily included with any Mass intention request.

A person of any religion may arrange for a Mass to be said, but it may feel awkward for someone who does not share the Catholic faith. Non-Catholics may prefer to send a memorial donation to a charity or organization that they feel more comfortable supporting. This donation should be in keeping with the wishes of the deceased and/ or the family, however, not just one's own church or favorite organization. A donation to the ASPCA, for example, when the deceased never showed much affection for animals, would not be nearly as welcome as a comparable donation to the charity designated by the survivors or one to which the deceased devoted much time and effort. If no memorials are specified, a personal check sent to the family may be appreciated. This may be used to defray funeral expenses, if necessary, or be added to a memorial gift of the family's choosing.

Taking food to the home of the bereaved is another time-honored custom in many communities, although I learned recently that this is not as universal a practice as I had previously assumed. Upon learning of the death, neighbors and friends prepare dishes that can be served to the relatives and close friends who will soon gather at the home of the deceased and/or the immediate survivor(s). Sometimes this is an organized gesture, as when a group of neighbors or co-workers plan a meal together. At other times, friends drop over individually with items that can easily be served and shared. Catholic dietary restrictions should not be a factor, unless we're bringing food on Friday. Meat is strictly prohibited only on Fridays during Lent (and Ash Wednesday), but some Catholics maintain the tradition of meatless Fridays throughout the year.

A few basic gestures can be offered and appreciated by mourners of any faith. Simply anticipating or recognizing the needs of the family and unobtrusively helping to meet them may alleviate some of the typical stress and chaos surrounding a death. For example, offering to help care for the youngest children, either at your home or the home of the bereaved, may free the parents and grandparents to focus on other tasks. Offering to meet out-of-town visitors at the airport and/or helping to arrange for their meals and accommodations is another thoughtful gesture, especially in large and widely-scattered families.

Under certain circumstances, helping to clean or tidy up the home of the deceased and/or the chief survivor(s) prior to the arrival of guests may be genuinely appreciated. Sometimes the weeks preceding death have been devoted to caring for a critically ill patient and routine housework has been understandably neglected. For some, the thought of friends and relatives seeing the home in such a state causes additional stress. Others may see it as a trivial concern.

With any offers of assistance, we must respect the family's privacy and their right to accept or reject any of our suggestions.

Preliminary Planning

Numerous people nowadays, especially the elderly, have taken steps to preplan their funeral arrangements. Anyone assisting in making funeral arrangements should, therefore, ascertain first whether the deceased may have left instructions regarding death. Presumably, any instructions of this kind and their location will have been made explicit to the likely survivor(s) ahead of time. Catholics who will be leaving primarily non-Catholic survivors may want to make sure their wishes regarding Catholic funeral practices are made known. (Incidentally, funeral information should not be recorded in the will, because that document ordinarily will not be read until after the burial.)

If no prearrangements have been made, the priest or his representative should be able to guide us through the necessary planning steps, outlining some of the options and explaining the preliminary decisions that need to be made. A "standard" Catholic funeral, as specified in the *Order of Christian Funerals* (promulgated in 1989), actually consists of three separate ceremonies: the Vigil Service, the Funeral Liturgy, and Committal. In addition, the *Order* suggests a rite for prayers immediately after death, a brief prayer service at the first gathering in the presence of the body (after it has been prepared for viewing), and again when the family and close friends prepare to accompany the body to the church or place of committal. There are several variations and possible combinations of these rites, however, so each funeral will be somewhat unique, depending on the needs and preferences of the family. In my own experience, some of these preliminary ceremonies are frequently omitted.

The Funeral Mass (or Funeral Liturgy, if a Mass is not desired) is the main liturgical service and should be the starting point around which other plans are made. Certain days (primarily Sundays during Advent, Lent, and the Easter season, Holy Days of Obligation, and Thursday, Friday, and Saturday during Holy Week) are prohibited for Catholic Funeral Masses, so dates may need to be adjusted accordingly. Usually, the Vigil Service takes place at the funeral home the evening before the funeral, although it can be arranged at the home of the deceased or at the church, also. The Rite of Committal customarily takes place at the cemetery, either at the gravesite or in an internment chapel on the premises.

The Wake

Though not mandated by Catholic custom or theology, contemporary American bereavement practices often involve calling hours at a funeral home for one or two days prior to the funeral.[8] This allows friends and extended family members to offer condolences to the immediate family. The casket is usually present, but may be either open or closed. Commonly called a wake, this time may be referred to as "visitation" or "viewing."

Historically, wakes were held at the dead person's home,[9] and that is still an acceptable, though less common, alternative to the funeral home. Some families prefer to receive visitors at their home, but leave the body elsewhere. Other families arrange for calling hours at the church, either with or without the casket in view. Specific arrangements often depend on the circumstances of death, the estimated number of visitors, and family preferences. Reliance on the funeral home setting also seems to differ somewhat by region and ethnic group as well.

If the wake does take place at a funeral home, much of the procedure will be "generic" and nonreflective of the deceased's religious affiliation. A few practices are specific to Catholics, however, and may be confusing to non-Catholic visitors. Similarly, Catholic callers at a non-Catholic wake may be surprised at the absence of certain familiar traditions.

One important distinction is the *prie-dieu* (a padded bench suitable for kneeling in prayer) located in front of the casket. When Catholic mourners and supporters visit the funeral parlor, it is customary to kneel on the *prie-dieu* for a few minutes praying for the deceased. Vigil lights and a crucifix are usually arranged near the casket to facilitate prayer. Non-Catholic visitors may kneel if they wish, but it is not necessary.

Another custom associated with Catholicism is the practice of having a commemorative holy card (also called a memorial card or prayer card) imprinted with an appropriate prayer or Scripture verse. The card includes the name of the deceased, his or her birth and death dates, and sometimes a photograph as well. Other times, a religious picture is featured in lieu of a photograph. These are usually displayed by the guest register book, and visitors may take a card home as a keepsake and as a reminder to pray for the departed.

In the past, I did not realize the significance attached to these memorial cards and treated them somewhat carelessly. Perhaps I mentally lumped them into the same category as imprinted napkins from weddings or inscribed matchbook covers from anniversary parties — inexpensive souvenirs of the day. Now that I have a better understanding of this practice, however, I know why devout Catholics often keep these holy cards tucked into Bibles or favorite prayer books. It is a tangible reminder of the deceased that encourages us continually to remember the departed in our prayers. Parents of young children may want to take extra cards to save and pass along to the children when they are old enough to participate in this discipline, also.

Visitors to a wake frequently wonder, "What should I say?" Often a simple "I'm sorry" is eloquent enough; our presence speaks for itself. Traditionally, visitors were expected to wait to speak to a mourner until the mourner spoke first. Today, this may not be strictly observed, but it's best to approach the survivor(s) silently. After the mourner greets us, either by word or gesture, we may offer condolences.

A few comments should be specifically avoided when speaking to Catholic mourners. Following death,

Protestants often speak with great certainty, saying, "We know he/she is in heaven now." As alluded to earlier, Catholic theology is more complex, and the exact state of the soul less assured in Catholic thinking. Though tempting to comfort the bereaved with such words, a more appropriate phrase may be "He/she certainly seemed to lead a faith-filled life," or some similar expression. When sincerely delivered, these words could bring comfort and reassurance to the bereaved Catholic without contradicting either party's religious beliefs.

Another comment that one sometimes hears at the funeral home is, "He/she looks almost alive," or the equally banal "Doesn't it seem as if he/she is just sleeping?" While these may attest to the skill of the undertakers, any comments that attempt to deny death or minimize the loss of life should be considered inappropriate.

Vigil Service

The evening before a funeral, Catholics customarily hold a vigil for the deceased. Prior to 1989, when the new *Order of Christian Funerals* was issued, families simply gathered and recited the Rosary together. That custom is still carried on in many families today. Recognizing that many non-Catholics feel uncomfortable with the Rosary, however, the *Order of Christian Funerals* suggests a Scripture-based vigil service. This service may be held at the funeral home toward the end of the visitation hours or at the church, either following calling hours or independent of them. It is usually led by a priest or deacon, although when no priest or deacon is available, a layperson may preside.[10] At times, the family may wish to have the vigil at the home of the deceased or bereaved instead. In this case, the format can be shortened and simplified, if desired.

Usually, the vigil service is open to anyone who wishes to attend, and the newspaper's death notice will include the time and place. Some people who will be unable to come to the funeral the next day may wish to attend the evening service. This gives them an opportunity to pray with the family in an organized way, in addition to offering personal condolences. Many, however, will attend both the vigil and the funeral service, especially family members and close friends.

The full vigil service includes Scripture readings, hymns, a short homily, prayers, and if desired, the recitation of the Rosary (although the *Order* itself does not mention it). The *Order of Christian Funerals* also suggests in the rubrics a time of family remembrance, where those gathered share with each other memories of the deceased. Depending on the size and formality of the gathering, this can either be done in an organized format with specific individuals asked in advance to prepare a few words, or more spontaneously, with everyone invited to reminisce in his or her own way.

This sharing of memories may also be arranged outside of the vigil service context, in a more informal way. Sometimes a display of mementoes or photos of the deceased helps trigger the reminiscing. When my brother-in-law passed away, the funeral home included an easel and felt boards for a photo display as part of the package. My sister-in-law and her children pored through boxes of photographs and arranged a beautiful display of photographs that touched many visitors to the funeral home. Nearly all who came found a picture of themselves or their friends or relatives that brought back fond memories.

Other personalized touches and informalities that would not be considered appropriate at a Funeral Mass can sometimes be included in the less formal vigil service. For example, songs or music that held special significance for the deceased, but are outside the traditional sacred music repertoire, might be effective during the vigil, especially when scheduled outside of the parish church setting.

When the vigil is held in the church, the introductory rites include the reception of the casket and the corresponding rituals. When the vigil is held elsewhere, these rites are omitted, forming the beginning of the funeral service the next day instead. (These are described in more detail below.)

Planning the Funeral

A priest can conduct the funeral liturgy either in the context of a Mass or outside of Mass, depending on family preference and the relationship of the deceased to the Church. A Funeral Mass, the preferred choice of most Catholic families, is customarily held in the parish church of the deceased or his/her family. In some dioceses, a Mass can occasionally be held at the funeral home, but in other dioceses Mass is limited to a church setting.

If many of the mourners are non-Catholic, the family may choose to have a funeral liturgy without a Mass to help them feel more comfortable with the service and to avoid any potential misunderstandings about Catholic Communion restrictions.[11] The liturgy outside of a Mass context may be conducted either at the funeral home or at church.

Regardless of which option we choose, family members can expect to play an active role both in planning and participating in the funeral. The principal ceremony planners are encouraged to select Scripture readings from among a number of appropriate choices and identify which hymns and music they wish to use. They also typically invite specific relatives or friends to serve as lectors, gift bearers, and Eucharistic ministers. While this liturgical planning may at times seem like an added burden to some survivors, such personalized touches can greatly enhance the beauty of the funeral ceremony and give added comfort to those in attendance.

If we are asked to assume one of these roles, we should consider it an honor and accept graciously. Some of us, however, may feel too overcome by grief to be able to read clearly or assist with the service on this occasion. In that case, we may suggest that someone who is a bit less emotionally involved be asked instead. The chief survivor should be able to respect our discomfort and find a suitable replacement. If no friends or family are willing to assume these roles, then trained members of the parish may be contacted.

At larger funerals, some mourners (usually six to ten) may be invited to serve as pallbearers. This may either be an honorary role (with the funeral home staff or other pallbearers actually lifting the casket), or a working role, where the duty of carrying the casket in and out of church falls to these selected friends and relatives. Traditionally, pallbearers have been men, but today women may also be asked to serve in this capacity (although it is still quite rare). Non-Catholics as well as Catholics may be pallbearers at a Catholic funeral. Similarly, Catholics may serve as pallbearers for a non-Catholic funeral whenever they are asked.

Unless the ceremony planner instructs otherwise, pallbearers wear dark suits (or dark dresses). This group customarily sits together during the funeral in the front of the church, so spouses and/or companions of pallbearers should expect to sit separately. Usually pallbearers are asked to arrive a bit early and meet with the priest and/or funeral home staff prior to the start of the service. If uncertain about genuflecting in the aisle or any other protocol, ask the priest or other knowledgeable person at this time.

Sometimes other friends and relatives may be asked to serve as ushers for the funeral. These people help seat the attendees, generally ensuring that the seats up front are filled first. (The very front pews, however, are always reserved for the immediate family.) At some funerals, the funeral home personnel may act as ushers. At others, no ushers are deemed necessary and visitors simply seat themselves.

Parish musicians usually have an established fee for their services. This may be paid directly by the family or paid by the funeral home and then billed to the family. For the priest and/or deacon, the family should have a stipend envelope prepared in advance, and a representative of the family can present it before or after the funeral services. (Sometimes the funeral home staff will deliver it upon request, also.) Again, stipend amounts vary widely across the country, but the typical range is probably from fifty to one hundred fifty dollars. The amount of time devoted to helping the family during the death and funeral process, as well as family circumstances, should be taken into account when determining a reasonable honorarium.

Additional Considerations

An additional planning consideration that arises in many families is, "What do we do with the children?" No clear-cut answers can be offered to this question because circumstances, family attitudes, and individual children vary so much. Some families may think it inappropriate for young children, grandchildren, or great-grandchildren to attend the funeral, while others will welcome the presence of the youngest generation. Similarly, some children will handle the death and its ceremonies with a maturity beyond their years, while other children may be traumatized by the sight of an open casket.

Decisions should be based on the age and maturity level of our children, how close they were to the deceased, and how we think the chief survivors may react to their presence. Sometimes it's difficult to determine whether the children will cope better by being included or excluded from the funeral rites. All we can do is use our best judgment and then continue to monitor the effects of grief after the funeral, offering as much support and reassurance as possible. As with other church services, we should take the children out any time they become too disruptive.

Parents of infants and toddlers may face limited options for child care, especially if they have traveled some distance to attend the funeral. When my husband's grandmother died, I remember struggling to keep my one-year-old out of trouble at the funeral home, struggling to keep him quiet during a Funeral Mass that coincided with his customary mealtime, and struggling to keep him warm at the cemetery. I would have preferred to leave him in someone else's care for a few hours, but the only people I knew in town were also attending the funeral. Staying home from the funeral to care for my child seemed an unacceptable alternative, since my absence would almost certainly have offended my in-laws.

In this type of situation, a neighbor or friend of the family could help immensely by offering to line up a reliable babysitter for out-of-town guests, or assuming child care responsibility personally, if attending the funeral does not take precedence. Making arrangements to use the church nursery or a semiprivate space at the funeral home to care for the younger children may also be a welcome gesture. Some families may prefer to keep the children with the parents, however, rather than leave them with someone unfamiliar during this time. We can approach the family with a clear offer of child-care assistance, then let them decide whether or not to accept our offer.

Another potentially troublesome issue that may need to be considered is whether or not cremation will be a factor in the funeral process. Until just recently, cremation posed particular concerns to Catholics, often complicating plans for a Catholic Funeral Mass and leaving priests and families at odds. Although the long-standing ban against cremation was lifted in 1963, ashes were still generally not permitted at Funeral Masses,[12] because Church law required that the urn or box containing the ashes be left outside the church (usually in a funeral car).

As one veteran pastor explained, "Priests were put in the awkward position of telling the families of the deceased they had to leave the remains at the curb."[13] In a situation where emotions are already running high, such a disagreement about how to handle the funeral can only compound the family's anguish and distress.

Recognizing that this was a growing problem for pastors and families, the United States bishops voted in June 1996 to ask the Vatican for a nationwide exception to this prohibition. While emphasizing that the ideal way to have a body cremated is to have it incinerated after the Funeral Mass, they also realize that the expense of transporting a body from a distant place of death to a funeral site often forces many people to ship the cremated remains back home instead. Checking with a priest *before* making any decisions about the disposal of a loved one's body should help minimize misunderstandings or conflict at the time of the funeral.

Another sensitive issue involves recording the funeral. Though I was unaware of the practice until researching this topic, some families or funeral homes apparently record the funeral either on audio or video for distribution to out-of-town guests who could not attend the services, or for family archival purposes. Perhaps in some cases, a recording of the event may be desirable (for example, where the surviving spouse in a traffic accident cannot leave the hospital and wants to view the funeral via tape), but many mourners are likely to be offended at the idea, regardless of who commissions it. Although news photographers seem to do it routinely, filming someone who is openly expressing grief still ranks as an invasion of privacy. I doubt that many Catholic priests would allow recording equipment at a funeral, except under compelling circumstances.

The Funeral

If the body has not already been received at the church as part of the vigil service, the rite of reception begins the Funeral Mass (or Funeral Liturgy). This is a simple yet beautiful rite, rich in symbolism. First the minister sprinkles the coffin with holy water "in remembrance of the deceased person's initiation and first acceptance into the community of faith."[14] Next, if it is the custom in the local community, the immediate family members, close friends, or the minister drape a white pall (a heavy cloth) over the casket. This, too, is reminiscent of the white baptismal garment and can be a way for the survivors to offer a final "service" to the deceased.

The entrance procession follows, including the ceremony participants and the pallbearers. Sometimes family members wish to place a Christian symbol or symbols on the pall, such as a Bible, a book of the Gospels, or a cross. If so, selected representatives of the family should carry these items in the procession, then lay them on the pall at the conclusion of the procession. Only Christian items are permitted in this ritual. Flags, organizational insignias, or secular items of any kind are not allowed on the casket, at least while it is in the church.

The funeral proceeds according to the standard Mass format, with Scripture readings, hymns, a homily, prayers, and Communion (or omitting Communion in the case of the funeral outside of Mass). At a Catholic funeral, the officiant's homily is supposed to speak about what Scripture tells us in general about death and resurrection, rather than focusing on the specific attributes or accomplishments of the deceased. Ideally, the pastor will be able to blend personal comments about the deceased into the broader context of a Christian life in his funeral homily. I have witnessed just that on several memorable occasions.

In an effort to make the Funeral Mass more personally meaningful to those gathered, a representative of the family may be asked to say something about the life of the deceased. The family decides who, if anyone, in addition to the clergy, may speak at the service. Unlike spontaneous reminiscences that may have been offered at the vigil service, this is a more formal speech, in keeping with the overall tone of the Mass or liturgy.

This spoken remembrance has been the target of much criticism and misunderstanding recently, largely because such remembrances have often detracted from, rather than added to, the funeral liturgy in the minds of many. Bishops around the country are now formulating tighter guidelines to restrict such talks at the funeral. In the Diocese of Fort Wayne-South Bend, Indiana, for example, current guidelines suggest that the vigil, the cemetery, or the consolation dinner are more appropriate places for such remembrances. If the family does elect to speak in remembrance at the Funeral Mass, local guidelines dictate that it must be a reflection on the life of the deceased in the context of his or her faith, that only one person should speak and not a series of people, that the talk should not exceed two minutes, and that the speaker review his or her written remarks with the presider in advance. In addition, they counsel against close family members speaking, because grief may make it difficult to be composed enough to speak clearly.[15] Although increasingly popular in some memorial venues, recordings and videos are not considered appropriate for a Catholic funeral liturgy.

After the remembrance, if there is one, a final commendation prayer and hymn conclude the funeral. As a farewell gesture and as a sign of respect or reverence, the priest incenses the casket. Holy water may be sprinkled also, although this is usually omitted if the casket was sprinkled during the rite of reception at the beginning of the Mass. The priest and assisting ministers then lead the procession out of the church, with the coffin, the family, and other mourners following.

Committal

The third and last ceremony outlined in the *Order of Christian Funerals* is the rite of committal. It may be celebrated at the grave, tomb, or crematorium, or even at sea. There are several variations of this rite, depending on whether it immediately follows the funeral or is celebrated independently of the funeral. (Sometimes a funeral is held in one city, for example, and burial in another.) It is basically a brief service of prayer, with perhaps a song at the end.

Where it is the custom, some sign or gesture of leave-taking may be made. Usually, this is done systematically with mourners queuing around the casket and placing flowers or soil on the coffin or simply placing a hand on the coffin in farewell. This procedure may be made clear ahead of time or we may just follow the lead of those for whom the custom is more familiar. Often the presiding minister makes an announcement that the family would like to invite everyone in attendance to some kind of meal immediately following.

The Funeral Meal

Friends and family rarely just disperse from the cemetery or the church, but gather together following the services to share memories of the deceased and enjoy a meal together. This may be at a restaurant, at the parish hall, at the home of the deceased, or at some other convenient location. When one of their fellow members dies, parishioners frequently prepare and serve food for the funeral dinner. (If a parish group provides a dinner after the funeral, an optional donation can be sent to the parish for that ministry, along with a thank-you note.) Other times, friends or neighbors may make meal arrangements for the guests. Sometimes the atmosphere at the funeral dinner may become quite jolly, as family and friends celebrate life in the midst of death.

After the Funeral

In the weeks following the funeral, the survivors write thank-you notes to those who have participated in the funeral service and those who offered various condolences. This task can be shared among the principal survivors and need not fall exclusively on one person. In the case of elderly survivors, another person (family or friend) can offer to assist in actually writing a note that the elderly person dictates. This is especially appreciated by those who may have a physical problem, such as arthritis, that makes writing painful. Family and friends should continue to remember the grieving both in prayer and in deed. Sometimes a short note, telephone call, or bouquet several weeks after the funeral means as much as or more to the survivors than those that are sent immediately.

Catholics have the additional obligation to remember the deceased, as well as the bereaved, in our thoughts and prayers. At each Mass, we pray not only for the living but also for those who have departed this life. One of the consoling factors of the Catholic faith is the belief that the communion of saints transcends death and allows us to maintain a connection with those who have gone before us. Our relationship with our loved ones changes significantly when death separates us, but the connection does not die.

Endnotes
1. "What Makes a Good Funeral?" *U.S. Catholic*, November, 2002, pp. 12-17.
2. *Order of Christian Funerals*, prepared by the International Commission on English in the Liturgy. Catholic Book Publishing Company, New York: 1989, no. 6.
3. For more information on the concept of purgatory, refer to the *Catechism of the Catholic Church*, nos. 1030-1032. Also, "The Sweet Pain of Purgatory," by Mark Shea in the September/October 1996 issue of *Catholic Heritage* (pp. 10-12), reviews current Church teaching on this topic.
4. These prayers are also listed in the *Order of Christian Funerals*.
5. See Gregory Young, *The High Cost of Dying*. Prometheus Books, Buffalo, N.Y.: 1994.

6. See *Catechism of the Catholic Church, Second Edition*, no. 2296, Libreria Editrice Vaticana, Citta del Vaticano: 1997. (Available from Our Sunday Visitor Publishing Division, Huntington, Ind.)

7. Several organizations that offer Masses for the deceased are: Sacred Heart Monastery, P.O. Box 900, Hales Corners, Wisc. 53130; The Spiritans, Holy Ghost Fathers, Brothers and Associates, 11411 Amherst Ave., Wheaton, Md. 20902; and Franciscan Missions Association, 274 West Lincoln Ave., Mt. Vernon, N.Y. 10551.

8. American families, however, do not follow this custom if they are Jewish. In the Jewish tradition, there is no pre-funeral visitation period, since burial typically takes place as quickly as possible, often within twenty-four hours of death. In many families, only the closest friends and family are expected to be at the funeral and graveside.

   The Shiva, or mourning period, begins immediately following the funeral. Family members will "sit shiva" at the home of the deceased or sometimes at the home of another family member, for up to seven days. Friends and relatives customarily make condolence calls at this time. It is appropriate to bring food (especially uncut fruit), but not flowers, to Jewish mourners. For more information, see Helen Latner's *The Book of Modern Jewish Etiquette*, Schocken Books: 1981.

9. The Hebrews began the idea of the Vigil for the Dead, or wake, as a means of guarding against premature burial. Family and friends stood watch for any signs of

life. The custom was continued by Christians in the Middle Ages as an act of piety. (This is taken from Ann Ball's *Catholic Book of the Dead*, Our Sunday Visitor Publishing Division, Huntington, Ind.: 1995, p. 47.)

10. See *Order of Christian Funerals*, no. 14.

11. Parish custom regarding reminders about Catholic Communion restrictions vary. Some pastors make an announcement; others omit any direct reference. The official policy as established by the National Conference of Bishops can be found on the inside cover of *Today's Missal: Masses for Sundays: Holy Days with Daily Mass Propers for the Liturgical Season*. Oregon Catholic Press. The *Catechism* reference is nos. 1398-1401.

12. In a few areas of the United States (Pueblo, Colo.; Reno, Nev.; and Honolulu, Hawaii) local bishops had requested and been granted a Vatican "indult," or permission, to overlook this stipulation.

13. Father James Setelik, quoted by Robert Holton in "To Comfort Mourners, New Cremation Rules." *Our Sunday Visitor*, July 21, 1996, p. 3.

14. *Order of Christian Funerals*, no. 133. As Michael Marchal notes in *Parish Funerals* (Liturgy Training Publications, Archdiocese of Chicago: 1987), "In the rites we inherited from the medieval church, holy water seemed to be used primarily for exorcism or absolution. Now it is a proclamation of the death and life into which the deceased entered through the waters of baptism."

15. See Diocese of Fort Wayne–South Bend, *Catholic Christian Funeral Guidelines*. September, 2001.